I0776365

The Story of a Special Day
Volume 263

September 19

The 262ⁿᵈ day of the year (263ʳᵈ in leap years). There are 103 days remaining until the end of the year.

by Michael Dobson

Timespinner
Press

This book is also available in e-book form for Kindle, e-pub devices, and other formats from your favorite online booksellers.

For more information about the series, about us, or about your special day, please email us at editor@timespinnerpress.com.

Look for other volumes in *The Story of a Special Day,* coming often. See www.timespinnerpress.com for details and for the most recent information.

Table of Contents

Cover: A pirate on deck, by Howard Pyle in Howard Pyle's Book of Pirates (1921), for **International Talk Like a Pirate Day** — the **Cover Story.**

Quote of the Day

"I am receiving what I suppose to be the usual number of threatening letters on the subject. Assassination can be no more guarded against than death by lightning; it is best not to worry about either."

James A. Garfield, 20th US President
assassinated September 19, 1881

Today
in
History
September 19

September, from the Brevarium Grimani

What Happened on September 19?

While some days of the year are more famous than others, every day of the year is filled with important, exciting, and unusual events, from religious awakenings to natural disasters, from wars to breakthroughs in technology, and from tragedy to triumph.

In this section, you'll learn about all the events that make September 19 important, including the special event that makes up our cover story or event of the day. Some events you may already know about, others may be new to you, but all of them are important parts of the history of the work.

Let's explore some of the reasons why September 19 is a very special day!

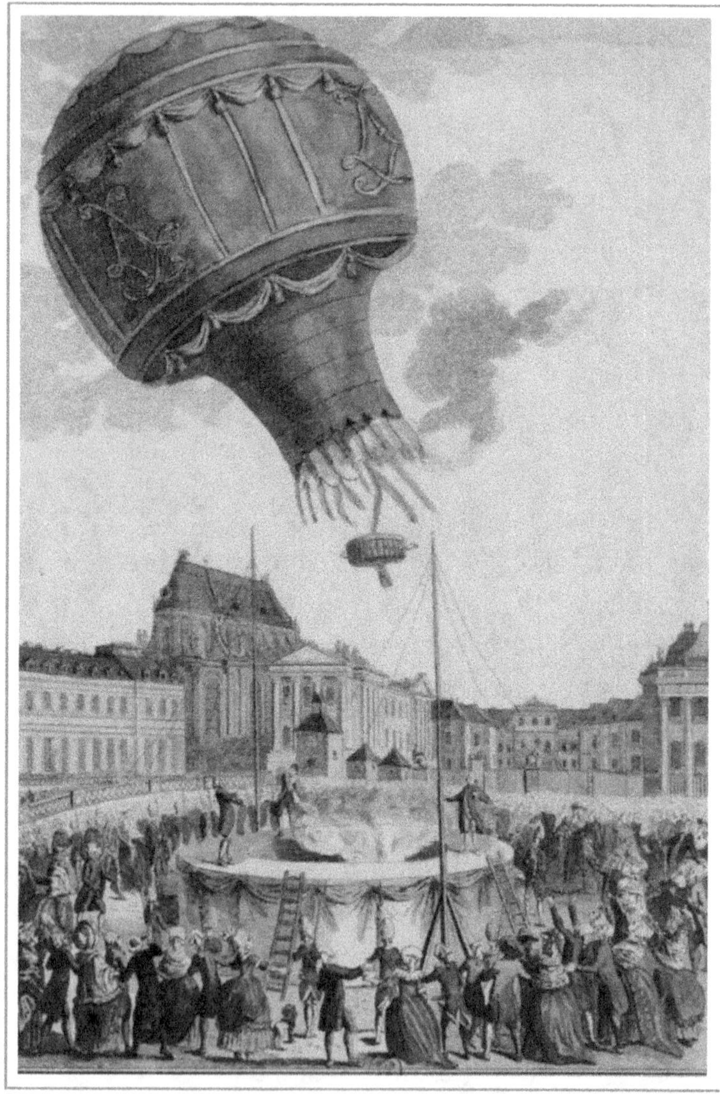

An illustration of the first balloon ascent carrying living beings

Event of the Day
First Live Balloon Ascent (1783)

The Montgolfier brothers, Joseph-Michel and Jacques-Étienne, invented the first hot air balloon. On September 19, 1783, they sent up the first living beings in their balloon: a sheep, a duck, and a rooster. The flight took eight minutes and covered three miles, reaching an altitude of about 1,500 feet.

Joseph-Michel and Jacques-Étienne were born to a wealthy family of paper manufacturers. Joseph-Michel was the twelfth child out of 16. He was known as a maverick and a dreamer.

Jacques-Étienne, the 15th child, was by contrast practical and businesslike, and eventually took over the family business. He and his brother made numerous technical innovations in paper manufacturing, including the first transparent paper and a self-acting hydraulic ram.

Jacques-Étienne Montgolfier

Joseph-Michel Montgolfier

Joseph-Michel was the first to become interested in aeronautics. He built parachutes and once jumped from the roof of the family house. One evening, while watching a fire, he noticed the embers flying up from the flames, and wondered how he could harness that force to allow travel in the air.

He built a box-like chamber out of thin wood and covered it with taffeta, and placed it on a stand over a fire. The box lifted off the stand and collided with the ceiling. Excited, he shared his discovery with Jacques-Étienne. They built a larger box and tried a test flight, but the box got away from them and crashed nearly two kilometers away.

After further experiments, the brothers designed a globe-shaped balloon made of sackcloth lined with paper, covered by a fishnet. On June 4, 1783, they flew their balloon in public for the first time, in an unmanned trip that lasted about ten minutes.

The next balloon, named *Aérostat Réveillon*, was significantly larger, 37,500 cubic feet (1060 m³) in capacity. It was made of taffeta coated with alum, painted blue and decorated with gold designs.

At the time, there was concern about the effects on people flying into the upper atmosphere. Louis XVI suggested sending up a couple of convicted criminals, but the brothers used animals instead.

The sheep (named Montauciel, or "Climb-to-the-sky") was selected because it was a mammal, expected to have a response similar to a human. The duck was chosen as a control, because it was already able to flight at height and would therefore not be affected. The rooster, a bird but one that did not fly, was another control.

The animals all survived, and the king allowed the brothers to test with humans. This time, the brothers built a 60,000 cubic foot (1,700 m^3) balloon, and on October 15, 1783, Jacques-Étienne became the first human to lift off from the Earth.

There are other claimants for the first to invent the hot air balloon, in particular a Brazilian Portuguese priest named Bartolomeu de Gusmão around 1709. Regardless, the pioneering Montgolfier brothers are unambiguously the first to demonstrate the ability to lift living creatures into the sky.

The first manned hot-air balloon (Credit: Claude-Louis Desrais)

Other September 19 Events

From the creation of great works of engineering and art, to devastating wars and natural disasters, thousands of years of history have left their mark on each and every day of the year. Here are some important events that occurred on September 19. (Illustrated items are shaded.)

1796 — George Washington's Farewell Address, an open letter to the citizens of the United States, is published.[*]

George Washington during his presidency, by John Trumbull

---

[*] You can read it at Wikisource.org under the name "Washington's Farewell Address."

1863 — American Civil War: The second day of the **Battle of Chickamauga,** the second bloodiest engagement of the war, takes place. It ends the following day with a Confederate victory.

The Battle of Chickamauga, by Alfred Waud

1868 — **La Gloriosa,** the Spanish Glorious Revolution, begins. At its end on September 27, Queen Isabella II will be deposed and a new king appointed; two years after that the monarchy is abolished and the first Spanish Republic is created.

1870 — The four-month **Siege of Paris** begins. It ends January 28, 1871, with a Prussian takeover of the city and the proclamation of the German Empire.

1879 — The **Blackpool Illuminations** are switched on for the first time in a tradition that lasts to the present day.

1893 — In a triumph for the **women's suffrage movement**, New Zealand women receive the right to vote.

1944 — The **Battle of Hürtgen Forest** between American and German forces begins. It will be the longest single battle ever fought by the US Army and the longest battle on German ground during the war. A German defensive victory and the beginning of the Battle of the Bulge results.

Shelter for HQ Company, 121st Infantry Regiment, during the **Battle of Hürtgen Forest** (Photo: US Army)

1982 — Computer scientist Scott Fahlman publishes the **first computer emoticon**, the typed "smiley."

```
19-Sep-82 11:44   From: Scott E Fahlman

I propose that the following character
sequence for joke markers:

:-)

Read it sideways. Actually, it is probably
more economical to mark things that are NOT
jokes, given current trends. For this, use

:-(
```

The message board post that originated the **emoticon**

1995 — The New York *Times* and the Washington *Post* publish the **Unabomber's manifesto**, eventually leading to his discovery and capture.

2010 — The *Deepwater Horizon* **oil spill** in the Gulf of Mexico, the largest marine oil spill in the history of the petroleum industry, is capped after four months.

Quote of the Day

"Aren't there any grownups at all?"

William Golding, author of *Lord of the Flies*
born September 19, 1911

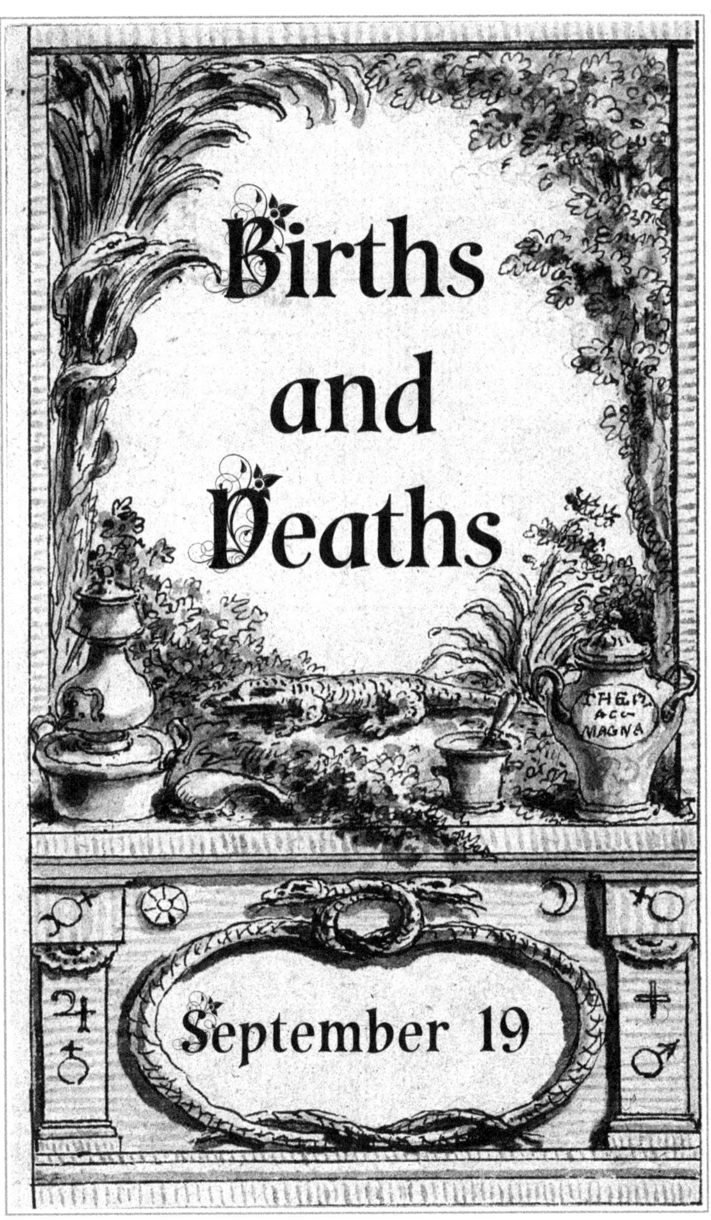

Births
and
Deaths
September 19

Adam West (right, as Batman) with Burt Ward (Robin) in the *Batman* television series. West was born September 19, 1928

Notable September 19 People

With the current world population at about seven billion people, on average about 19 million people also celebrate their birthdays on September 19 — and that isn't counting millions and millions who came before! No matter when you were born, you share your birthday with many special people whose accomplishments (and occasionally embarrassments) have been noted as part of history.

In this section, you'll meet fascinating people who share your birthday. They're organized by what they're famous for, and then in reverse chronological order from most recent to earliest. Those who are shown in photographs or artwork have a box around them. We don't have photos of everyone, so please forgive us if your favorite person is missing.

Some of these people you've heard of, others will be new to you, but they all make up an important part of the reason that September 19 is a truly special day!

                                        Michael Dobson

"The Three Bears," by **Arthur Rackham**, from Flora Annie Steel's
English Fairy Tales (1918)

Who Was Born on September 19?

Art and Illustration

Arthur Rackham, noted illustrator of books, especially in the field of fantasy literature. *(1867)*

Business and Technology

Ferdinand Porsche, automobile designer and son of the founder of Volkswagen and Porsche; head of the company following World War II. *(1909)*

A Porsche 356, designed by **Ferdinand Porsche.** (Photo: Roger and Renate Rössing for Deutsche Fotothek, CC BY-SA 3.0)

Fashion and Food

Michael Symon, celebrity chef who appeared on *Iron Chef America* and *Food Feuds.* *(1969)*

Mario Batali, celebrity chef who hosted the Food Network show *Molto Mario. (1948)*

Twiggy, supermodel and "swinging sixties" cultural icon known for her androgynous look. *(1949)*

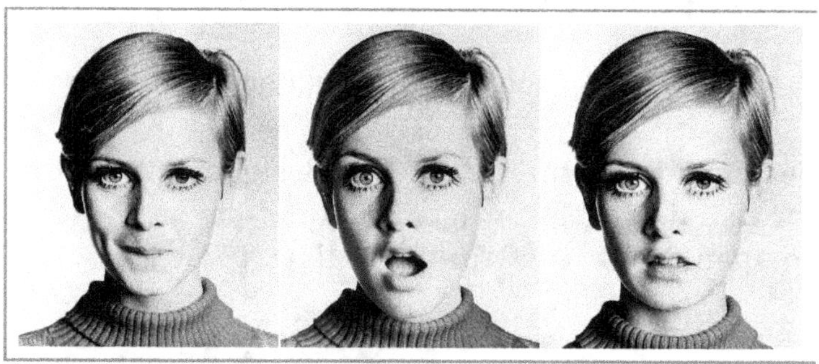

Twiggy (Photo: Amarylllis Sternweiser, CC BY-SA 2.0)

Government and Law

Barry Scheck, attorney on O. J. Simpson's defense team in the "trial of the century;" co-founder of the Innocence Project, championing those wrongfully convicted of crimes. *(1949)*

Lewis F. Powell, Jr., associate justice of the US Supreme Court from 1971 to 1987. *(1907)*

Leon Jaworski, second Watergate Special Prosecutor following the "Saturday Night Massacre" firing of his predecessor under the orders of President Richard Nixon. *(1905)*

Antoninus Pius, emperor of Rome from 138 to 161. Considered one of the Five Good Emperors of the Nerva-Antonine Dynasty along with his predecessor Hadrian, his successor Marcus Aurelius, Nerva, and Trajan. *(86)*

Journalism and History

Soledad O'Brien, television journalist known as an anchor of *American Morning, Starting Point,* and other news programs. *(1966)*

Joan Lunden, television journalist who co-hosted ABC's *Good Morning America* for seventeen years. *(1950)*

Mike Royko, Chicago newspaper columnist best known for *Boss,* his negative biography of Mayor Richard Daley, which won the 1972 Pulitzer Prize for Commentary. *(1932)*

Sarah Louise Delany, first African-American permitted to teach domestic science at a high school level in New York publish schools; along with her sister she was the subject of the bestselling oral history *Having Our Say,* by Amy Hill Hearth. she lived to be 103 years old. *(1889)*

Literature

Tanith Lee, British author of over 90 novels in science fiction, horror, and fantasy; first woman to win the British Fantasy Award for Best Novel. *(1947)*

Stefanie Zweig, German writer whose 1995 bestselling autobiographical novel *Nirgendwo in Afrika* was adapted into an Academy Award for Best Foreign Language Film movie. *(1932)*

Damon Knight, science fiction author and critic whose best known story, "To Serve Man," was adapted as an episode of *The Twilight Zone*; member of the Science Fiction Hall of Fame. *(1922)*

William Golding, author of the classic *Lord of the Flies*; received the 1983 Nobel Prize for Literature . *(1911)*

Military and Adventure

Sunita Williams, astronaut who set records for most total spacewalks by a woman and most spacewalk time for a woman; commander of Expedition 33 to the International Space Station. *(1965)*

Benjamin Hacker, first US Navy flight officer to be promoted to rear admiral. *(1935)*

Thomas Cavendish, led the first deliberate expedition to circumnavigate the globe. *(1560)*

William Golding (Courtesy Dutch National Archives, CC BY-SA 3.0)

RADM Benjamin Hacker (US Navy)

Sunita Williams (left) with Michael Lopez-Alegria putting on their extravehicular mobility units prior to a spacewalk (Courtesy NASA)

Music

Candy Dulfer, saxophonist who has performed with numerous artists including Prince and Dave Stewart; nominated for a Grammy for her first album, 1990's *Saxuality. (1964)*

Trisha Yearwood, country music artist whose hits include "She's in Love With the Boy," "Walkaway Joe," and "I Would've Loved You Anyway." *(1964)*

Lita Ford, lead guitarist for The Runaways before embarking on a solo career. *(1958)*

Freda Payne, singer best known for the 1970 hit "Band of Gold." *(1942)*

"Mama" Cass Elliot, singer and actress inducted into the Rock and Roll Hall of Fame as a member of the Mamas & the Papas; vocalist on "California Dreamin'," "Monday, Monday," and "Dream a LIttle Dream of Me." *(1941)*

Paul Williams, musician and actor who wrote such hits as "An Old Fashioned Love Song," "We've Only Just Begun," and "Rainy Days and Mondays," as well as the theme song for the TV series The Love Boat. Appeared in films including *Smokey and the Bandit* and *Phantom of the Paradise.* *(1940)*

The Mamas and the Papas on *The Ed Sullivan Show,* 1968. From left to right: Michelle Phillips, **Cass Elliot,** Denny Doherty, and John Philips. Cass Eliot was born September 19, 1941

Paul Williams

Sylvia Tyson, part of the folk duo Ian and Sylvia; best known song is "You Were On My Mind." *(1940)*

The folk duo Ian and Sylvia in 1968. **Sylvia Tyson** (with guitar, foreground) and husband Ian Tyson

Bill Medley, singer-songwriter and half of The Righteous Brothers, whose hits include "You've Lost That Lovin' Feeling" and "Unchained Melody." *(1940)*

Brian Epstein, music entrepreneur best known as the manager of the Beatles. *(1934)*

Brook Benton, singer-songwriter whose hits include "It's Just a Matter of Time," "Endlessly," and "Rainy Night in Georgia." *(1931)*

Nick Massi, bass singer and bass guitarist for The Four Seasons; member of the Rock and Roll Hall of Fame. *(1927)*

Helen Carter, country music singer best known as a member of The Carter Family. *(1927)*

Billy Ward, founded the R&B vocal group the Dominoes, known for their 1951 hit "Sixty Minute Man," considered one of the first rock and roll records. *(1921)*

Helen Ward, singer with the Benny Goodman Orchestra and other swing bands. *(1913)*

Performing Arts

Alison Sweeney, best known for her role as Sami Brady on *Days of Our Lives. (1976)*

Jimmy Fallon, host of *The Tonight Show Starring Jimmy Fallon* beginning in 2014 and long-time cast member of *Saturday Night Live. (1974)*

Sanaa Latham, actress known for starring roles in *The Best Man* and *Alien vs. Predator*; received the NAACP Image Award for Outstanding Actress for her role in *Love & Basketball. (1971)*

Victor Williams, actor best known for playing Deacon on the sitcom *The King of Queens. (1970)*

Cheri Oteri, cast member on *Saturday Night Live* from 1995 to 2000. *(1962)*

Rex Smith, former teen idol who starred in the 1985 television series *Street Hawk* and who performed the 1979 hit single, "You Take My Breath Away.". *(1955)*

Jeremy Irons, stage and screen actor who won a Best Actor Oscar for 1990's *Reversal of Fortune*; Batman's butler in DC superhero films beginning with 2016's *Batman v. Superman. (1948)*

Robert Mantooth, actor on the 1970s medical drama *Emergency!* who became a spokesperson for firefighter and EMS workers. *(1945)*

David McCallum, best known for playing Illya Kuryakin in *The Man from U.N.C.L.E.* and "Ducky" Mallard in *NCIS. (1933)*

Adam West, best known for playing the title role on the 1960s TV series *Batman. (1928) (Photo page 18.)*

William Hickey, nominated for an Academy Award for playing Don Corrado Prizzi in 1985's *Prizzi's Honor. (1927)*

Rosemary Harris, Tony-winning stage actress best known for playing Aunt May in Sam Raimi's *Spider-Man* trilogy; mother of actress Jennifer Ehle; member of the American Theatre Hall of Fame. *(1927)*

Jeremy Irons

David McCallum in *The Man From U.N.C.L.E.*

James Lipton, best known as the producer and host of the television show *Inside the Actors Studio. (1926)*

Don Harron, best known as the KORN newscaster Charlie Farquharson on the country music and comedy show *Hee Haw. (1924)*

Frances Farmer, co-starred with such actors as Bing Crosby and Cary Grant; committed involuntarily to a mental hospital with a diagnosis of paranoid schizophrenia. Her story was told in the 1982 film *Frances,* starring Jessica Lange. *(1913)*

Porter Hall, actor whose best known roles included a senator in *Mr. Smith Goes to Washington* and the psychologist who tests Kris Kringle in *Miracle on 34th Street. (1888)*

Ben Turpin, actor and comedian in the vaudeville and silent film eras; known for his physical comedy. *(1869)*

1921 American Caramel Company promotional card of **Ben Turpin**

From left: actresses Martha Scott, Uta Hagen, **Frances Farmer,** and Julie Haydon (Credit: Alfredo Valente, *Stage* magazine, 1938)

Science

Masatoshi Koshiba (小柴 昌俊), Japanese astrophysicist who shared the 2002 Nobel Prize for Physics for the detection of cosmic neutrinos and other neutrino research. *(1926)*

William Kirby, English parson and naturalist considered the founder of the field of entomology. *(1759)*

Sports

Aleksandr Karelin (Александр Карелин), considered the greatest Greco-Roman wrestler of all time with a career record of 887 wins and two losses. Won gold medals in three Olympic games under three different flags (Soviet Union, Unified Team, and Russia along with nine World Championships and twelve European championships. *(1967)*

Jim Abbott, baseball pitcher who played ten seasons in the MLB even though he was born without a right hand. Won the James E. Sullivan Award as the best US amateur athlete while at the University of Michigan and played on the US baseball team that won gold in the 1988 Olympics. *(1967)*

David Seaman, English football (soccer) goalkeeper who was awarded an MBE for his services to football. *(1963)*

William Kirby, by T. H. Maguire

Jim Abbott

Ken Rosenthal, sportswriter and reporter who served as lead reporter for *Major League Baseball on Fox*. *(1962)*

Joe Morgan, second baseman for two World Series championship teams during a career that ran from 1963 to 1984; member of the Baseball Hall of Fame. *(1943)*

Jim Fox, British pentathlete who won a gold medal in the 1976 Olympics. *(1941)*

Al Oerter, American discus thrower who was the first athlete to win a gold medal in the same event in four consecutive Olympics. *(1936)*

Duke Snider, center fielder primarily for the Brooklyn and Los Angeles Dodgers from 1947 to 1962; member of the Baseball Hall of Fame. *(1926)*

Willie Pep, world featherweight boxing champion during the period 1947 to 1950; member of the International Boxing Hall of Fame. *(1922)*

Al Oerter (Photo: Angelo Cozzi/Mondadori)

"Fishermen Launching a Rowing Boat," by **Michael Ancher**

"The Lifeboat is Taken Through the Dunes," by **Michael Ancher**

Who Died on September 19?

Art and Photography

Eddie Adams, photojournalist who took the Pulitzer Prize-winning 1969 photograph of a South Vietnamese police chief executing a Vietcong prisoner on the streets of Saigon. *(2004)*

Eddie Adams' 1968 Pulitzer Prize-winning photograph "General Nguyen Ngoc Loan executing a Viet Cong prisoner in Saigon" (Copyright © 1968 Wide World Photos)

Michael Ancher, Danish painter known for his paintings of fishermen. *(1927)*

Business and Finance

Hiroshi Yamauchi (山内 溥), turned Nintendo from a small playing card company to a global video game conglomerate. *(2013)*

Orville Redenbacher, businessman and entrepreneur best known as the co-founder and public face of Orville Redenbacher brand popcorn. *(1995)*

Orville Redenbacher

Condé Montrose Nast, publisher and entrepreneur who founded magazine publisher Condé Nast, whose magazines included *Vogue, House & Garden, Vanity Fair, Glamour, The New Yorker, GQ, Wired,* and many others. *(1942)*

Mayer Amschel Rothschild, founded the Rothschild banking dynasty; named by *Forbes* as one of the most influential businessmen of all times. *(1812)*

Crime and Punishment

Giles Corey, accused of witchcraft along with his wife Martha during the Salem witch trials. He was tortured in an attempt to force him to plead guilty or not guilty to the charges. His wife was hanged three days later. *(1692)*

Giles Corey being pressed with heavy stones to force him to enter a plea. Because he died without entering a plea, his children were able to inherit his estate rather than have it confiscated by the state.

Government and Politics

James A. Garfield, 20th President of the United States and the second president to be assassinated. Only sitting member of the House of Representatives ever elected President; he was an advocate of civil rights and civil service reform. He was shot by disappointed job seeker Charles Guiteau on July 2, 1881. Although the gunshot did not kill him, the wound became infected and led to his death *(1881)*

Literature and Poetry

Jackie Collins, romance novelist whose 32 novels all appeared on the New York *Times* bestsellers list; sister of actress Joan Collins. *(2015)*

Italo Calvino, Italian journalist and author of the *Our Ancestors* trilogy and *Invisible Cities;* received numerous awards, including the French Legion of Honor, the Austrian State Prize for European Literature, and the World Fantasy Life Achievement Award. *(1985)*

Masaoka Shiki (正岡 子規), considered one of the great masters of the haiku and a major influence on modern haiku. He also played baseball, and was inducted into the Japanese Baseball Hall of Fame. *(1902)*

James A. Garfield (Photo: Mathew Brady and Levin Handy)

Music and Dance

Chuck Rio (Danny Flores), rock saxophonist best known for writing and performing the 1958 hit "Tequila." *(2006)*

Skeeter Davis, country and pop singer whose hits include "Set Him Free," "(I Can't Help You) I'm Falling Too," and "The End of the World." *(2004)*

Slim Dusty, country music singer-songwriter and guitarist who was the first Australian to have a number one international hit song (1957's "A Pub With No Beer"); named an Australian National Treasure. *(2003)*

Hermes Pan, dancer and choreographer best known as Fred Astaire's long-time collaborator on 17 films. *(1990)*

Gram Parsons, singer-songwriter and guitarist known as a member of The Byrds and The Flying Burrito Brothers. *(1973)*

Red Foley, country music singer and member of the Grand Ole Opry whose hits included "Peace in the Valley," "Chattanoogie Shoe Shine Boy," and "Birmingham Bounce." Member of the Country Music Hall of Fame. *(1968)*

Gram Parsons

Red Foley

Performing Arts

Audrey Long, actress in such films as *Tall in the Saddle, Born to Kill,* and *Desperate;* wife of Leslie Charteris, who created the mystery character The Saint. *(2014)*

Dolores Hope, best known as the wife of comedian Bob Hope. *(2011)*

Elizabeth Allen, actress in such films as *Donovan's Reef, Diamond Head, and Cheyenne Autumn,* and in television roles including *The Twilight Zone, The Jackie Gleason Show,* and *The Paul Lynde Show. (2006)*

Ann Doran, actress best known for playing James Dean's mother in 1955's *Rebel Without a Cause. (2000)*

Patricia Hayes, actress whose films include *The NeverEnding Story, A Fish Called Wanda,* and *Willow. (1998)*

Pamela Brown, stage and screen actress whose film roles include *Lust for Life, Cleopatra, Becket,* and *A Funny Thing Happened on the Way to the Forum. (1975)*

Science and Engineering

Chester Carlson, inventor of the xerography process that led to the creation of the Xerox copier. *(1968)*

Konstantin Tsiolkovsky (Константи́н Циолко́вский), pioneering Russian rocket scientist considered one of the founding fathers of modern rocketry and astronautics. *(1935)*

Konstantin Tsiolkovsky

Gaspard-Gustave de Coriolis, French
mathematician and engineer who developed the
mathematical underpinnings for what is now known
as the Coriolis force. *(1843)*

Gaspard-Gustave de Coriolis, by Zéphyrin Belliard

Ole Rømer, Danish astronomer who made the first
quantitative measurements of the speed of light,
invented the modern thermometer, developed and
installed the first street lights in Copenhagen, and
invented various astronomical and navigation
devices. *(1710)*

Sports

Willie Steele, won a gold medal for the long jump in the 1948 Olympic Games; member of the National Track and Field Hall of Fame. *(1989)*

Ole Rømer, by Jacob Coning

Quote of the Day

"There comes a point when a dream becomes reality and reality becomes a dream."

Frances Farmer, actress
born September 19, 1913

Holidays
Around
the World

September 19

                                    Michael Dobson

International Talk Like a Pirate Day founders Mark Summers ("Cap'n Slappy") and John Baur (Ol' Chumbucket)

International Talk Like a Pirate Day inspiration **Robert Newton** (left) in the title role in the 1952 film *Blackbeard the Pirate,* with Linda Darnell

September 19 Events

If you're looking for a reason to take your special day off, you should know that every single day is a holiday somewhere in the world! Here's some of what you can celebrate on September 19!

Cover Story
International Talk Like a Pirate Day

Ahoy, matey! On International Talk Like a Pirate Day, that's how to say hello. Around the world, people talk like pirates ("Arrr!"), dress like pirates, and celebrate a romanticized view of pirate life.

As far as we can tell, International Talk Like a Pirate Day is the only holiday to come into being as a result of a sports injury, specifically a 1995 racquetball game between Oregonians John Baur and Mark Summers. One of them was injured, and yelled, "Aaarrr!" And with that, International Talk Like a Pirate Day came into being.

Although the fateful game took place on June 6, Baur and Summers chose September 19 (the birthday of Summer's ex-wife) for the annual celebration out of respect for the D-Day landings. They wrote a letter about their holiday to syndicated humor columnist Dave Barry, who liked the idea and began promoting it. Today, thanks to growing media coverage, it is celebrated internationally.

Of course, real pirates sounded nothing like movie pirates. What we think of as "pirate speech" is actually the native accent of English actor Robert Newton, who played Long John Silver in Disney's

1950 film *Treasure Island* and a 1954 film *Long John Silver*, as well as the title character in 1952's *Blackbeard the Pirate.*

Newton was born in the southwest English town of Dorset and educated in Cornwell, and used his native West Country dialect to portray his pirate characters. In the West Country dialect, for example, "Arrr" (or "Yarrr") means yes.

Pirates have existed nearly as long as there's been trade by sea. The Sea Peoples in the 14th century BCE menaced civilizations in the eastern Mediterranean Sea. Pompey the Great fought pirates in the Mediterranean Sea during the time of Julius Caesar, who was himself kidnapped by pirates and held for ransom. The Vikings conducted raids throughout Western Europe during the Middle Ages.

The Barbary Corsairs even had their own mini-nations, and in the early years of American independence the US government paid nearly 20% of its annual expenditures to the Barbary states for protection. Modern pirates operate in the Persian Gulf, eastern Africa, and southeast Asia.

Our romanticized view of pirates originates in the Golden Age of Piracy, which lasted from around 1650 to 1730 and focused on the Caribbean Sea. Famous pirates included Henry Morgan, William "Captain" Kidd, Edward "Blackbeard" Teach, and "Calico Jack" Rackham and his partner Anne Bonny.

Real pirates weren't very nice people, but fictional ones can be fun. Avast, ye scurvy knaves! It's time to celebrate International Talk Like a Pirate Day!

Long John Silver, by N. C. Wyeth, from Robert Louis Stevenson's *Treasure Island* (1911) — for **International Talk Like a Pirate Day**

General Events

Independence Day (Saint Kitts and Nevis)
The Caribbean nation of Saint Kitts and Nevis observes its September 19, 1983, independence from the United Kingdom.

Brimstone Hill Fortress, Saint Kitts, a UNESCO World Heritage Site — **for Saint Kitts and Nevis Independence Day** (Photo: Martin Falbisoner, CC BY-SA 4.0)

Deň 1. Verejného Vystúpenia SNR (Slovakia)
Slovakia observes a Remembrance Day for the first public appearance of the Slovak National Council, which occurred September 19, 1848.

Día de las Glorias del Ejército (Chile)
Chile celebrates *Fiestas Patrias* (Native Land Holidays) on September 18 and 19. The 19th is known as the "Day of the Glories of the Army."

Food Days

In the United States, almost every day of the year is dedicated to a particular food. (Some other countries also have official food days, but only in America is there one every single day!) Sponsored by manufacturers, retailers, farmers, or simply fans, these days are often proclaimed by the President, Congress, state governors, or mayors. Given that there are more different foods than days of the year, some days honor more than one kind of food!

In the US, September 19 is **National Butterscotch Pudding Day.**

The word "pudding" comes from a Latin word meaning "small sausage." While US puddings are usually sweet, savory puddings (Yorkshire pudding, black pudding) can be found around the world.

Butterscotch Pudding (Photo: Stacy Spensley, CC BY-SA 2.0) — for **National Butterscotch Pudding Day**

The earliest appearance of butterscotch dates to mid-19th century Yorkshire. Modern butterscotch is made primarily of brown sugar and butter, and is sometimes served in the form of hard candies, and as a sauce for ice cream.

A butterscotch pudding is a type of blancmange. Blancmange is made with cream or milk and sugar thickened with cornstarch, and usually served cold. With butterscotch flavor added, it becomes butterscotch pudding.

Food Months

The entire month of September is used to celebrate numerous foods. Here's a list of what to eat this month!

- Bourbon Heritage Month
- California Wine Month
- National Chicken Month
- National Honey Month
- National Mushroom Month
- National Papaya Month
- National Potato Month
- National Rice Month
- National Whole Grains Month
- National Wild Rice Month

A glass and bottle of bourbon, for **Bourbon Heritage Month**
(Photo: Dirk Ingo Franke, CC BY-SA 4.0)

Jars of honey at the NC State Fair 2009, for **National Honey Month**
(Photo: Jo Anna Barber, CC BY-SA 2.0)

Religious Feast Days and Holidays

Feast of San Gennaro
(Italian communities in the US)

Beginning in September 1926, immigrants from Naples in the Little Italy section of Manhattan, congregated along Mulberry Street to celebrate **Januarius**, the Patron Saint of Naples, whose feast day is September 19.

The celebration has grown, with other Feasts of Gennaro held in the Bronx, New Jersey, Los Angeles, and Las Vegas. The Los Angeles event was founded by talk show hosts Jimmy Kimmel and Adam Carolla.

The famous scene in *The Godfather Part II*, in which young Vito Corleone stalks and kills his rival, happens during the Feast of San Gennaro.

Feast of San Gennaro (2014) (Photo: MusikAnimal, CC BY-SA 3.0)

Saint Januarius, by Caravaggio

Saint Days

Each day in the year is considered a feast day for one or more saints. They are somewhat different in western Christianity (Catholicism and many forms of Protestantism) and in eastern (Orthodox) Christianity.

In *Western Christianity,* September 19 is the feast day of Saints Alonso de Orozco Mena; Goeric of Metz; Januarius; Our Lady of La Salette; Theodore of Tarsus; and Trophimus, Sabbatius, and Dorymedon.

In *Eastern Orthodox Christianity,* it is also the commemoration of Saints Zosimas of Cilicia, Felix and Constantia, Eustochius, Seguanos, Pomposa, and David and Constantine. (These saints are honored on September 6 by "Old Calendrists†.")

---

† "Old Calendrists" use the older Julian calendar for liturgical purposes rather than the modern Gregorian one. See "What Day of the Week is September 19?" for the differences between the Julian and Gregorian calendars.

Non-Gregorian Religious Events

Not every culture uses the familiar Gregorian calendar, so some events may shift days or months over the years. Here is a selection of primarily religious events around the world that sometimes take place on September 19.

- Aadi Perukku (Tamil calendar, Hinduism)
- Anant Chaturdashi (Hindus and Jains)
- Binara Poya (Buddhism)
- Chaturmas (Hindu calendar, also observed in Jainism, Buddhism)
- Gai Jatra (Nepali calendar)
- Ghanta Karna (Nepali calendar)
- Jhulan Purnima (Hindu calendar)
- Kumbh Mela (Hindu calendar)
- Nag Panchami (Hindu calendar)
- Onam (Malayalam Calendar, Hinduism)
- Pitru Paksha (Hinduism)
- Raksha Bandhan (Hindu calendar)
- Rosh Hashanah LaBehema (Judaism)
- Shravana Putrada Ekadashi (Hindu calendar)
- Teejdi 3rd day of Raksha Bandhan (Hindu calendar)
- Varalakshmi Vratam (Hindu calendar)
- Vassa (Theravada Buddhism)

Honorary Months and Moveable Celebrations

Nations around the world issue proclamations recognizing particular months to honor certain causes. If not otherwise specified, all months are US. Here are some honorary designations for September.

- Baby Safety Month
- Be Kind to Editors and Writers Month
- Children's Good Manners Month
- College Savings Month
- Happy Cat Month
- International Square Dancing Month
- National Preparedness Month
- National Recovery Month
- National Service Dog Month
- National Yoga Month
- Pain Awareness Month
- Responsible Dog Ownership Month

Two Young Cats, by Julius Anton Adam, **for Happy Cat Month**

Moveable and Multi-Day Events

Some events take place over a specific week or time period. Some events occur on different days each year (such as "fourth Saturday of a month"). These events sometimes take place on or include September 19. All are US unless otherwise specified.

Second Saturday

- Day of the Workers in the Oil, Gas, Power, and Geological Industry (Turkmenistan)
- National Iguana Awareness Day
- Prairie Day

An iguana in the Galapagos (Photo: Simon Matzinger, CC BY-SA 4.0) — for **National Iguana Awareness Day**

Second Sunday

- Auditor's Day (Scientology)
- Father's Day (Latvia)
- National Grandparent's Day (Canada, Estonia)
- National Pet Memorial Day
- Tanker's Day (Russia)

First Sunday after the first Monday

- National Grandparent's Day (United States)

Nearest Weekday to September 12

- Saragarhi Day (Sikhism)

Visiting Grandmother, Felix Schlesinger — for **National Grandparent's Day**

A boy wearing a backpack, for **School Backpack Awareness Day** (Photo: Robert Michael, CC BY-SA 2.5)

Just for Fun

Anybody can make up a holiday, and many people do! While none of these are officially recognized and some may come and go, here are a few more holidays for September 19.

- International Drive Your Studebaker Day (2nd Saturday)
- School Backpack Awareness Day (3rd Wednesday)

A 1961 Studebaker Hawk in the Netherlands (Photo: Alf van Beem) — for **International Drive Your Studebaker Day**

Quote of the Day

"O sweet September, thy first breezes bring
The dry leaf's rustle and the squirrel's laughter,
The cool fresh air whence health and vigor spring
And promise of exceeding joy hereafter."

George Arnold, *September Days*

About
the
Month
of
THER.M
ACU
MAGNA
September

"September," by Eugène Grasset

September: The Ninth Month

The morrow was a bright September morn;
The earth was beautiful as if new-born;
There was that nameless splendor everywhere,
That wild exhilaration in the air,
Which makes the passers in the city street
Congratulate each other as they meet.

Henry Wadsworth Longfellow, "Tales of a Wayside Inn"

In Latin, *septem* means "seven," so it may seem strange that September is actually the *ninth* month of the year. The original Roman calendar, on which ours is based, started in March, making September indeed the seventh month. No one is completely sure when the start of the year was moved to January, but the traditional name of September stuck.

Romans also associated September with the god Vulcan, and thus expected the month to have fires, volcanic eruptions, and earthquakes.

In the northern hemisphere, September marks the beginning of meteorological autumn. In the southern hemisphere, September is the seasonal equivalent of March, the beginning of spring.

September and December always begin on the same day of the week. However, no other month in the same year will end on the same day of the week as September.

For countries that switched from the Julian to the Gregorian calendars in 1752, the date jumped from September 2 to September 14, meaning that September 3 through 13 don't exist in that year.

September in Other Cultures

In Old English, the month of September was known as *Hāligmōnaþ*. Anglo-Saxons called it *Gerst monath* (Barley month) celebrating the barley harvest that would shortly be turned into beer.

In Finland, it is *syyskuu*, in Poland *wrzesień*, and in Greece *Σεπτέμβριος*. The Russians call the month *сентябрь*.

While both the Hebrew and Arabic cultures have their own calendar system, the Hebrew word for "September" is ספטמבר and in Arabic it's سبتمبر.

The Azerbaijani call the month *Sentyabr*.

In Hindi, the month of "sitambar" is written सतिंबर.

In both China and Japan, it's known as 九月, 구월 in Korea, and 腩尯 in Vietnam.

Afternoon in September, Frank Weston Benson

September Symbols

Birthstone: Sapphire, representing clear thinking.

Star sapphire

Birth Flowers: Forget-me-not, morning glory, and aster.

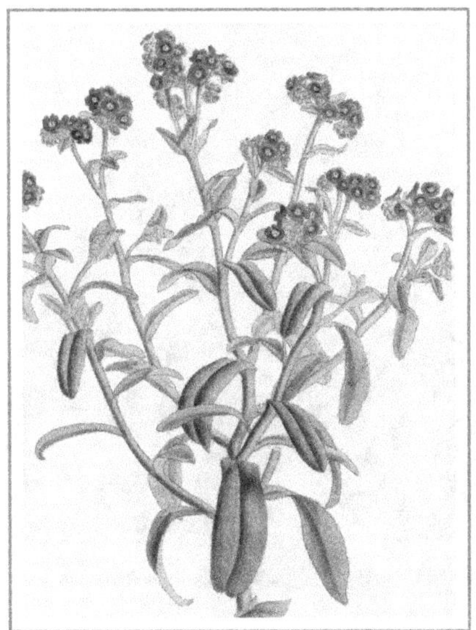

Forget-me-not (*moyosotis azorica*)

September Sayings and Superstitions

Here are some wedding sayings and superstitions associated with the month of September.

- "Marry in September's shrine, your living with be rich and fine."
- "A September bride will be discreet, affable, and much liked."
- "Married in September's golden glow / Smooth and serene your life will go."

As for which day of the week, that's easy.

Monday for health, Tuesday for wealth,
Wednesday best of all, Thursday for losses,
Friday for crosses, Saturday for no luck at all.

A Regency wedding proposal

September, by Joachim von Sandrart

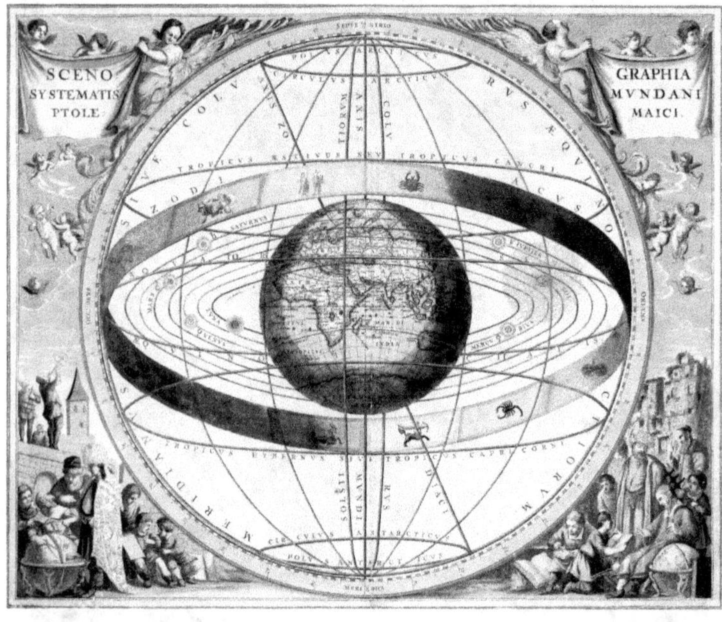

Scenography of the Ptolemaic Cosmography, by Johannes van Loon, based on Andreas Cellarius's *Harmonia Macrocosmica*, 1660

September 19 Zodiac Signs

From the perspective of someone on Earth, the Sun appears to move through the sky throughout the year, along a path astronomers call the *ecliptic plane*. The ecliptic plane is divided into twelve constellations, known as the zodiac, based on traditionally observed patterns of stars. On your birthday, you can't see your constellation, because it's in the daytime sky.

The zodiac was first developed by Babylonian astronomers about 2,500 years ago. Because they were unaware that the Earth wobbles like a spinning top (known as *precession*), they didn't make allowance for the fact that the Sun's path through the zodiac changes over time.

That means there are now two sets of dates for your birth sign. The *tropical dates* are the original Babylonian dates; the *sidereal dates* tell you where the Sun actually appears as it moves along its annual path.

September 19, however, is one of the few days in the year in which both the tropical and the sidereal sign is the same: **Virgo.**

Virgo

Tropical August 23 to September 23
Sidereal September 16 to October 15

The constellation of Virgo was originally associated with the grain harvest and symbolized fertility. The Greeks and Romans saw Virgo as Demeter or Ceres, the goddess of agriculture. In art, Virgo is often represented as carrying two sheaves of wheat. In the Middle Ages, Virgo was also sometimes connected to the Virgin Mary.

In astrology, Virgos are associated with being observant, helpful, and reliable, but can be perceived as inflexible and cold. They are supposed to be compatible with Taurus, Cancer, and Capricorn, but not with Gemini, Libra, or Aries.

Zodiac, by Alphonse Mucha

Illustration by Edward Penfield

What Day of the Week is September 19?

On what day of the week does September 19 fall?

Surprisingly, this isn't an easy question. Because the calendar year is 365 days long (366 in leap years), it doesn't divide evenly by the seven days of the week.

Also, the Earth goes around the Sun in about 365-1/4 days, so a calendar tends to drift over time. That's why the same date falls on different weekdays in different years.

This is made even more complicated by a change in calendars that took place in 1582. Our modern calendar has its roots in ancient Rome, in a calendar reform conducted by Julius Caesar. Caesar commissioned mathematicians to attack the problem, and they came up with the idea of leap years, and thus standardized the calendar for centuries to come. This was called the Julian calendar.

Over time, however, the small errors in Caesar's calculation compounded. That's why Pope Gregory XIII commissioned the Gregorian calendar, used in most of the world today. Some countries converted in 1582, when the calendar was first developed; some converted later; other still haven't changed.

Gregorian and Julian aren't the only types of calendars. The Hebrew year, the Islamic year, and many other calendars are used in different parts of the world and among different people.

You can convert Gregorian dates to other calendars, including the Hebrew calendar, the Islamic calendar, and even the Mayan calendar by visiting the Fourmilab Calendar Converter at http://www.fourmilab.ch/documents/calendar/.

Chinese calendar systems are quite complex and have changed several times; a full discussion is far beyond the scope of this book. If you're interested, you can find information here: http://www.hermetic.ch/cal_stud/chinese_cal.htm.

On Names and Dates

Historians use "CE" (Common Era) and "BCE" (Before the Common Era) instead of the more common "AD" (Anno Domini, or Year of Our Lord) and "BC" (Before Christ), reflecting the fact that the year-numbering system established by the Gregorian calendar is used throughout the world in many countries not culturally Christian.

The CE/BCE designation dates back to at least 1708, and has been adopted as a standard by the United Nations and the Universal Postal Union. Because this series of books covers events and people of all nations and cultures, we use the CE/BCE terms.

The abbreviation "O.S." ("Old Style") and "N.S." ("New Style") on some dates refers to the fact that the Russian Empire (in particular) did not switch from the Julian to the Gregorian calendar at the same time as the rest of Europe, and therefore some figures and events have two dates.

Also, in the Julian calendar in England in the 16th century, the year began on March 25 rather than January 1. To avoid confusion with Gregorian dates, dates between January and March were often written using both years.

People and events whose original names are not in the Western alphabet have their native names (where possible) in the appropriate script shown in parenthesis. If you are using an e-reader to access an electronic version of this book, all characters don't always display on all devices.

A 50-year brass perpetual calendar.

Quote of the Day

"Time is an illusion, lunchtime doubly so."

Douglas Adams,
from *The Hitchhiker's Guide to the Galaxy*

Notes
and
Credits

Timespinner
Press

Cartoon by John T. McCutcheon

Copyright, Credit, and Contact

Follow Us

Our blog "This Day in History" (http://timespinnerpress.com/this-day-in-history/) features short articles on events and people associated with each day, and updates several times each week. Also subscribe to the "Quote of the Day" at http://timespinnerpress.com/quote-of-the-day/. You can get daily links by following us on Facebook at TimespinnerPress, or on Twitter as @sidewisethinker.

Contact Us

Find an error or a format problem? Want information about the series, about us, or about when the volume for your special day might be available? Please email us at editor@timespinnerpress.com. (We also take requests if your special day isn't yet complete. Please give us at least six weeks' notice if possible.)

Sources

We owe a great debt to Wikipedia, which is our first stop for research. We attempt to make independent confirmation of all important dates and facts through a variety of other sources.

Other sources we frequently use include the Library of Congress; "on this day" listings from *Encyclopedia Britannica*, the *New York Times*, and the BBC; Omniglot for the names of months in other languages; *Chase's Calendar of Events*; and, of course, the always essential Google.

All art and photographs are either in the public domain, used under a Creative Commons license, or with a "fair use" justification, and most frequently come from Wikimedia Commons and the Library of Congress Prints and Photographs Division.

Attribution is provided where possible, or as requested by the copyright owner, or when there is particular historical significance, listed below. For information about any particular illustration or photograph, please contact us.

Credits

1. The cover illustration of Captain Keitt on deck is by Howard Pyle, and first appeared on a color plate facing page 212 in the 1921 book *Howard Pyle's Book of Pirates: Fiction, Fact, and Fantasy Concerning the Buccaneers and & Marooners of the Spanish Main* (New York and London: Harper and Brothers). It is in the public domain because it first appeared prior to January 1, 1923, and its copyright has expired.

2. The illustration of the month of September used on the back cover is from the French Gothic illuminated manuscript *Les Très Riches Heures du duc de Berry* by the Limbourg Brothers, Jean Colombe, and an intermediate painter whose name is lost to history. It is in the public domain because its copyright has expired.

3. The box graphic used on the first page is from a 1916 pamphlet entitled "Divorce versus Democracy" authored by G. K. Chesterton, originally published in London by the Society of St. Peter and St. Paul. It is in the public domain in the US because it was published prior to 1923, and is in the public domain in all countries (including the country of origin) in which the copyright time is the author's life plus 70 years or less.

4. The graphic design for the section pages in this book is from a design originally created for a pharmacy label. It is courtesy of Wellcome Images (ICV No 11073, photo V0010813), and is used here under CC BY-SA 4.0.

5. The painting *September* is from the *Brevarium Grimani*, circa 1510, and is in the public domain because its copyright has expired.

6. The 18th century illustration of the first balloon flight carrying living beings is in the public domain because its copyright has expired.

7. The 18th century portrait of Jacques-Étienne Montgolfier is in the public domain because its copyright has expired.

8. The portrait of Joseph-Michel Montgolfier first appeared in the 1887 book *Histoire des ballons et des aéronautes célèbres* by Gaston Tissandier (Paris: H. Launette & Cie.). It is in the public domain because its copyright has expired.

9. The 1783 illustration of the first manned hot-air balloon is by Claude-Louis Desrais, and is in the public domain because its copyright has expired.

10. The 1793 painting of George Washington by John Trumbull is in the public domain because its copyright has expired. It is in the collection of the Harvard Art Museums.

11. The 1863 drawing from the Battle of Chickamauga by Alfred Waud is from the Library of Congress Prints and Photographs Division (digital ID ppmsca.21066). It is in the public domain because its copyright has expired.

12. The 1945 photograph from the Battle of Hürtgen Forest is in the public domain as a work created by an employee of the US government as part of that person's official duties.

13. The 1982 message from Scott Fahlman is believed to be in the public domain.

14. The 1966 publicity photograph from the television series *Batman* is in the public domain because it was first published in the United States between 1923 and 1977 without a copyright notice. Traditionally, publicity photographs are not copyrighted because of the way in which they are intended to be used.

15. The illustration of the Three Bears by Arthur Rackham appeared in the 1918 book *English Fairy Tales*, by Flora Annie Steel (London: Macmillan). It is in the public domain because its copyright has expired.

16. The 1954 photograph of the Porsche 356 was taken by Roger and Renate Rössing for Deutsche Fotothek, who holds the copyright. It is part of a collection made available to Wikimedia Commons by Deutsche Fotothek, who has licensed it under CC BY-SA 3.0 Germany. The image has been cropped.

17. The photograph of Twiggy was taken by Amaryllis Sternweiser (flicker.com/8216275065), and is used here under CC BY-SA 2.0.

18. The 1983 photograph of William Golding is courtesy of the Dutch National Archives (Nationaal Archief) and Spaarnestad Photo, and is used here under CC BY-SA 3.0 Netherlands.

19. The 2007 photograph from ISS Expedition 14 is in the public domain as a work created by NASA.

20. The official US Navy photograph of Benjamin Hacker is in the public domain as a work created by an employee of the US government as part of that person's official duties.

21. The 1968 publicity photograph from the *The Ed Sullivan Show* is in the public domain because it was first published in the United States between 1923 and 1977 without a copyright notice. The image has been cropped.

22. The 1974 publicity photograph of Paul Williams is in the public domain because it was first published in the United States between 1923 and 1977 without a copyright notice.

23. The 1968 publicity photograph of Ian and Sylvia is in the public domain because it was first published in the United States between 1923 and 1977 without a copyright notice.

24. The 2014 photograph of Jeremy Irons was made available by Irons' publicist under CC BY-SA 3.0.

25. The 1965 publicity photograph of David McCallum in *The Man from U.N.C.L.E.* is in the public domain because it was first published in the United States between 1923 and 1977 without a copyright notice.

26. The 1921 American Caramel Company promotional card of Ben
    Turpin is in the public domain because it was first published in the
    United States prior to January 1, 1923.
27. The scanned photograph by Alfredo Valente from *Stage* Magazine,
    June 1938 issue (Vol. 15, No. 9, pg. 9), is in the public domain
    because it was first published in the United States between 1923 and
    1963, and although there was a copyright notice, the copyright was
    not renewed.
28. The 1998 photograph of Jim Abbott was released by John Traub,
    general manager of the Albuquerque Isotopes, under CC BY-SA 3.0.
29. The 1851 illustration of William Kirby by T. H. Maguire is in the
    public domain because its copyright has expired.
30. The 1960 photograph of Al Oerter is by Angelo Cozzi for Mondadori
    Publishers. It is in the public domain in Italy, its country of origin,
    because its copyright has expired, and in the United States because
    it was published before 1978 and was out of copyright in Italy on
    the URAA date of restoration.
31. The 1881 painting "Fishermen Launching a Rowing Boat" by
    Michael Ancher is in the Skagens Museum, Denmark, by way of
    Google Art Project. The image is in the public domain because its
    copyright has expired.
32. The 1883 painting "The Lifeboat is Taken Through the Dunes" by
    Michael Ancher is in the National Gallery of Denmark, Copenhagen,
    by way of Google Art Project. The image is in the public domain
    because its copyright has expired.
33. The Associated Press photograph "General Nguyen Ngoc Loan
    executing a Viet Cong prisoner in Saigon" by Eddie Adams is
    copyright © 1968 Wide World Photos. It is used here under "fair
    use" provisions of the US copyright code. It is necessary to identify
    the photojournalist in a biographical entry, no free equivalent is
    available, its use here does not limit the copyright holder's rights to
    distribute the image in any way, and it is a low-resolution image
    unsuitable for the production of counterfeit goods.
34. The 1979 publicity photo of Orville Redenbacher is in the public
    domain because it was first published in the United States between
    1978 and 1989 without a copyright notice, and its copyright was not
    subsequently registered with the US Copyright Office within five
    years of publication.
35. The circa 1923 illustration of Giles Corey first appeared in *Cyclopedia
    of Universal History* by John Clark Ridpath. It is in the public domain
    because it was first published in the United States between 1923 and
    1963, and although there may or may not have been a copyright
    notice, the copyright was not renewed.
36. The photograph of James A. Garfield was taken by Mathew Brady
    and Levin Handy between 1870 and 1880, and is in the public

domain because its copyright has expired. It is from the Brady-Handy Photo Collection at the Library of Congress (digital ID cwpbh.03744).

37. The 1972 publicity photograph of Gram Parsons is in the public domain because it was first published in the United States between 1923 and 1977 without a copyright notice.

38. The 1944 photograph of Red Foley appeared in the *Billboard 1944 Music Yearbook*. It is in the public domain because it was first published in the United States between 1923 and 1977 without a copyright notice.

39. The photograph of Konstantin Tsiolkovski is in the public domain because its copyright has expired. It is from the Memorial Museum, Feucht, Germany.

40. The 1841 engraving of Gaspard-Gustave de Coriolis by Zéphyrin Belliard is in the public domain because its copyright has expired.

41. The painting of Ole Rømer by Jacob Coning was created circa 1700, and is in the public domain because its copyright has expired.

42. The 2005 photograph of Mark Summers and John Baur is licensed under the CC BY-SA 3.0 license. The name of the photographer is unknown.

43. The screenshot from the trailer for the 1952 film *Blackbeard the Pirate* is in the public domain because it was first published in the United States between 1923 and 1977 without a copyright notice. Traditionally, film trailers are not copyrighted because of the way in which they are intended to be used, although the films themselves are.

44. The 2016 photograph of the Brimstone Hill Fortress on Saint Kitts is copyright © Martin Falbisoner, and is used here under CC BY-SA 4.0.

45. The 2015 photograph of bourbon is copyright © Dirk Ingo Franke, and is used here under CC BY-SA 4.0.

46. The 2009 photograph of jars of honey is copyright © Jo Anna Barber, and is used here under CC BY-SA 2.0.

47. The 2014 photograph of the Feast of San Gennaro is copyright © MusikAnimal, and is used here under CC BY-SA 3.0.

48. The painting *Saint Januarius Shows His Own Relics* is believed to be a copy of a lost work by Michelangelo Merisi da Caravaggio, and can be found at the Palmer Art Museum, Pennsylvania State University. As it was created between 1610 and 1612, it is in the public domain because its copyright has expired.

49. The painting of cats by Julius Anton Adam was created circa 1882 and is in the public domain because its copyright has expired.

50. The 2014 photograph of a Galapagos land iguana is copyright © Simon Matzinger. It is used here under CC BY-SA 4.0.

51. The painting *Bei Großmutter* by Felix Schlesinger was created prior to 1910 and is in the public domain because its copyright has expired.

52. The 2005 photograph of a boy carrying a backpack is copyright © Robert Michael, and is used here under CC BY-SA 2.5.

53. The 2009 photograph of a Studebaker Hawk is by Alf van Beem, who released the image into the public domain under CC0 1.0.

54. The 1896 illustration *September* by Eugène Grasset is in the public domain because its copyright has expired.

55. The 1913 painting *Afternoon in September* by Frank Weston Benson is in the public domain because its copyright has expired. It is in the collection of the National History Museum of Los Angeles County.

56. The photograph of a star sapphire was released into the public domain by its author, Mitchell Gore.

57. The chromolithograph of a forget-me-not is by Louis-Aristide Léon Constans and originally appeared in the 1852-1853 edition of *Paxton's Flower Garden*. It is in the public domain because its copyright has expired.

58. The painting *September* by Joachim von Sandrart is in the public domain because its copyright has expired. The original can be found in the Staatsgalerie im Neuen Schloss, Schleißheim, Germany.

59. The celestial sphere is from *Scenography of the Ptolemaic Cosmography,* by Johannes van Loon, based on Andreas Cellarius's *Harmonia Macrocosmica*, 1660. It is in the public domain because its copyright has expired.

60. The illustration "Zodiac" by Alphonse Mucha is in the public domain in the Czech Republic, its country of origin, and in all other areas in which the copyright term is the author's life plus seventy years or less.

61. The 1906 automobile calendar is by Edward Penfield, and is in the collection of the Library of Congress Prints and Photographs Division. It is in the public domain because its copyright has expired.

62. The 50-year perpetual calendar photograph is in the public domain.

63. The cartoon by John T. McCutcheon is from his 1905 collection *The Mysterious Stranger and Other Cartoons by John T. McCutcheon*. It is in the public domain because its copyright has expired.

64. The detail from the painting *Augsburg Labours of the Months: Autumn*, by Jörg Breu the Elder was created prior to 1550, and is in the public domain because its copyright has expired. The painting is in the Deutches Historisches Museum, Berlin.

65. The painting *September* by Hans Thoma is from his book *Festkalender*. It is in the public domain because its copyright has expired.

License Description and Terms

Aside from material purely in the public domain, photographs and other material in this book are used under specific licenses permitting free use, usually with an attribution requirement. For full text and terms of these licenses, click or enter the appropriate links below. If you believe there is an error in the copyright status or attribution of any of these images, please email us.

- Creative Commons Attribution 2.0 Generic (CC-BY 2.0): http://creativecommons.org/licenses/by/2.0/deed.en

- Creative Commons Attribution-Share Alike 3.0 Generic (CC-BY-SA 3.0): http://creativecommons.org/licenses/by-sa/3.0/

- Creative Commons Attribution-Share Alike 2.5 Generic (CC-BY-SA 2.5): http://creativecommons.org/licenses/by-sa/2.5/deed.en

- Creative Commons Attribution-Share Alike 2.0 Generic (CC-BY-SA 2.0): http://creativecommons.org/licenses/by/2.0/deed.en

- Creative Commons Attribution-Share Alike 1.0 Generic (CC-BY-SA 1.0): http://creativecommons.org/licenses/by-sa/1.0/deed.en

- CC0 1.0 Universal (CC0 1.0) Public Domain Dedication (CC0 1.0) http://creativecommons.org/publicdomain/zero/1.0/deed.en

- GNU Free Documentation License (GFDL): http://en.wikipedia.org/wiki/Wikipedia:Text_of_the_GNU_Free_Documentation_License

- License Art Libre (Free Art License): http://artlibre.org

"September," detail from *Augsburg Labours of the Months: Autumn,* by Jörg Breu the Elder (Courtesy Deutches Historisches Museum, Berlin)

Other Books from Timespinner Press

Timespinner
Press

The Story of a Special Day

Michael Dobson

A series of (eventually) 366 volumes covering everything that happened on your special day! Events, births, deaths, quotes, holidays, and much more. It's like a birthday card they'll never throw away!

US$7.95 print / US$2.99 ebook.

From Plassey to Pakistan

Humayun Mirza

The history of British Colonial India and the formation of Pakistan from the unique perspective of the son of Pakistan's first president and last of the royal line of Bengal, Bihar, and Orissa! This unique historical document tells the inside story of this distinguished family, including the detailed story of the coup that toppled his father from power!

US$27.95 print

A Whole New Navy: America's War in the Pacific

Miles Durr

The most comprehensive and detailed description of America's naval war in the Pacific ever—every battle, every ship, every task force and every task group from Pearl Harbor through the Japanese surrender! A must-have for the collection of every World War II buff!

US$29.95 print

Improbable History: The Weird, the Obscure, and the Strangely Important

edited by Michael Dobson

From the birth of Western civilization to the rescue of Apollo 13, from the Leaning Tower of Pisa to Florence's Duomo, history has often turned on small, improbable details. Whatever happened to the ancient Samaritan people? Why did a fortuitous rainstorm allow the British to conquer India? How did an air raid in Italy lead to the development of chemotherapy? What happened when Albert Einstein met Adolf Hitler on the streets of Berlin? How did the Japanese manage to attack the US mainland using balloons? A cast of award-winning writers tackle some of the strangest tales in history!

US$19.95 print

The Letters of William Philip Schwartz 1842-1855

edited by John F. Schwartz

The 19th century soldier and adventurer William Philip Schwartz wrote a series of vivid and detailed letters chronicling his adventures in the Indian Wars, the Mexican-American War, the Gold Rush, and his term as Marine sergeant aboard the USS Constellation. A pioneer in photography, he took *the first known war photographs*. An unforgettable first-hand look into life in the 19th century!

US$17.95 print

Watergate Considered as an Organization Chart of Semi-Precious Stones (and other essays)

by Michael Dobson

In this light-hearted yet insightful tour through the Nixon White House, the Committee to Re-Elect the President, and the various investigative committees, you'll meet fascinating characters from Richard Nixon himself to such lieutenants as a G. Gordon Liddy and John Dean. You'll gain insights into the origin of the scandal, the motives of the players, and how the situation spiraled so badly out of control.

US$9.95 print/US$3.99 ebook

  Michael Dobson

September, by Hans Thoma